[redacted]

What Kind of Clouds?

By NADIA HIGGINS
Illustrations by SARA INFANTE
Music by ERIK KOSKINEN

CANTATA LEARNING

WWW.CANTATALEARNING.COM

CANTATA
LEARNING

Published by Cantata Learning
1710 Roe Crest Drive
North Mankato, MN 56003
www.cantatalearning.com

Library of Congress Control Number: 2017007521
978-1-68410-061-3 (hardcover/CD)
978-1-68410-099-6 (paperback)

What Kind of Clouds? by Nadia Higgins
Illustrated by Sara Infante
Music Erik Koskinen

Book design, Tim Palin Creative
Editorial direction, Flat Sole Studio
Executive musical production and direction, Elizabeth Draper
Music arranged and produced by Erik Koskinen

Printed in the United States of America in North Mankato, Minnesota.
072017 0367CGF17

ACCESS THE MUSIC!
SCAN CODE WITH MOBILE APP
CANTATALEARNING.COM

TIPS TO SUPPORT LITERACY AT HOME

WHY READING AND SINGING WITH YOUR CHILD IS SO IMPORTANT

Daily reading with your child leads to increased academic achievement. Music and songs, specifically rhyming songs, are a fun and easy way to build early literacy and language development. Music skills correlate significantly with both phonological awareness and reading development. Singing helps build vocabulary and speech development. And reading and appreciating music together is a wonderful way to strengthen your relationship.

READ AND SING EVERY DAY!

TIPS FOR USING CANTATA LEARNING BOOKS AND SONGS DURING YOUR DAILY STORY TIME

1. As you sing and read, point out the different words on the page that rhyme. Suggest other words that rhyme.
2. Memorize simple rhymes such as Itsy Bitsy Spider and sing them together. This encourages comprehension skills and early literacy skills.
3. Use the questions in the back of each book to guide your singing and storytelling.
4. Read the included sheet music with your child while you listen to the song. How do the music notes correlate to the words of the song?
5. Sing along on the go and at home. Access music by scanning the QR code on each Cantata book. You can also stream or download the music for free to your computer, smartphone, or mobile device.

Devoting time to daily reading shows that you are available for your child. Together, you are building language, literacy, and listening skills.

Have fun reading and singing!

There are many kinds of clouds. Some are white and fluffy. Others are thin and gray.

Clouds can help you to tell what the weather will be like. But no matter what kind of clouds are floating up in the sky, all clouds are made of water droplets.

Turn the page to learn all about the different kinds of clouds. Remember to sing along!

Clouds are water. It's that simple.
Vapor floats up in the sky.

Tiny drops and icy **crystals**
form the sky shapes **drifting** by.

Are they gray or white, fluffy or thin?
What kind of clouds will this day bring?

A stratus cloud!

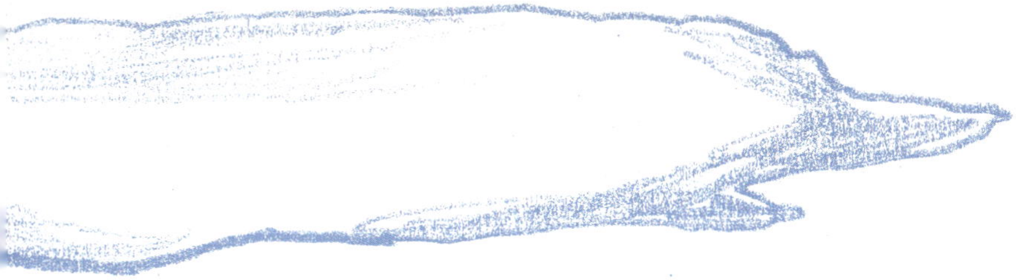

Like a blanket, this cloud lies
low and thin across the sky.

Watch it **drizzle**, oh, so gray.
Settle in for a cozy day.

Clouds are water. It's that simple.
Vapor floats up in the sky.

Tiny drops and icy crystals
form the sky shapes drifting by.

Are they gray or white, fluffy or thin?
What kind of clouds will this day bring?

A cirrus cloud!

So high above and icy white,
it sparkles in the bright sunlight.

Thin and **wispy** as a feather,
cirrus promises fair weather.

Clouds are water. It's that simple.
Vapor floats up in the sky.

Tiny drops and icy crystals
form the sky shapes drifting by.

Are they gray or white, fluffy or thin?
What kind of clouds will this day bring?

A cumulus cloud!

White and **puffy**, it drifts through
a sky so perfectly blue,
shifting fast from shape to shape—
a cat, a dragon, now an ape!

Clouds are water. It's that simple.
Vapor floats up in the sky.

Tiny drops and icy crystals
form the sky shapes drifting by.

Are they gray or white, fluffy or thin?
What kind of clouds will this day bring?

A cumulonimbus cloud!

Towering tall and flat on top,
this storm cloud is ready to pop.

Flash! Crack! Growl! Ka-BOOM!
Thunder and lightning shake the room.

Are they gray or white, fluffy or thin?
What kind of clouds will this day bring?

SONG LYRICS
What Kind of Cloud

Clouds are water. It's that simple.
Vapor floats up in the sky.
Tiny drops and icy crystals
form the sky shapes drifting by.

Are they gray or white, fluffy or thin?
What kind of clouds will this day bring?

A stratus cloud!
Like a blanket, this cloud lies
low and thin across the sky.
Watch it drizzle, oh, so gray.
Settle in for a cozy day.

Clouds are water. It's that simple.
Vapor floats up in the sky.
Tiny drops and icy crystals
form the sky shapes drifting by.

Are they gray or white, fluffy or thin?
What kind of clouds will this day bring?

A cirrus cloud!
So high above and icy white,
it sparkles in the bright sunlight.
Thin and wispy as a feather,
cirrus promises fair weather.

Clouds are water. It's that simple.
Vapor floats up in the sky.
Tiny drops and icy crystals
form the sky shapes drifting by.

Are they gray or white, fluffy or thin?
What kind of clouds will this day bring?

A cumulus cloud!
White and puffy, it drifts through
a sky so perfectly blue,
shifting fast from shape to shape—
a cat, a dragon, now an ape!

Clouds are water. It's that simple.
Vapor floats up in the sky.
Tiny drops and icy crystals
form the sky shapes drifting by.

Are they gray or white, fluffy or thin?
What kind of clouds will this day bring?

A cumulonimbus cloud!
Towering tall and flat on top,
this storm cloud is ready to pop.
Flash! Crack! Growl! Ka-BOOM!
Thunder and lightning shake the room.

Are they gray or white, fluffy or thin?
What kind of clouds will this day bring?

What Kind of Clouds?

Americana
Erik Koskinen

Chorus

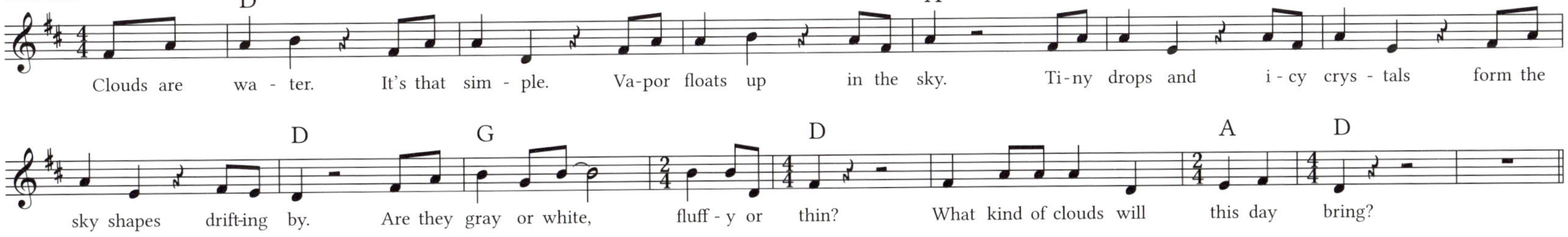

Verse

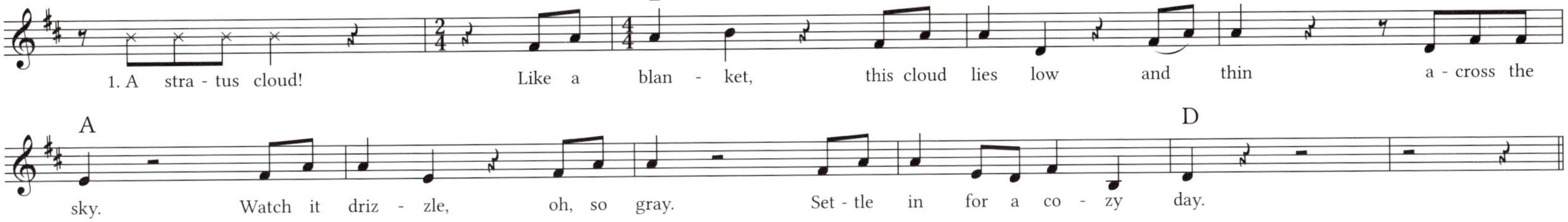

Chorus

Verse 2
A cirrus cloud!
So high above and icy white,
it sparkles in the bright sunlight.
Thin and wispy as a feather,
cirrus promises fair weather.

Chorus

Verse 3
A cumulus cloud!
White and puffy, it drifts through
a sky so perfectly blue,
shifting fast from shape to shape—
a cat, a dragon, now an ape!

Chorus

Verse 4
A cumulonimbus cloud!
Towering tall and flat on top,
this storm cloud is ready to pop.
Flash! Crack! Growl! Ka-BOOM!
Thunder and lightning shake the room.

Outro

GLOSSARY

crystals—glass-like substances with many see-through sides

drifting—slowly moving

drizzle—rain that falls lightly in very small drops

puffy—rounded and airy

shifting—changing from one thing to another

towering—rising to a tall height

vapor—tiny droplets of water floating in the air

GUIDED READING ACTIVITIES

1. Look outside. What kind of clouds do you see in the sky? What kind of weather are you having?

2. The next time you go outside, look up. Can you see any shapes in the clouds? What shapes do you see?

3. Draw an outdoor scene. Include one of the clouds from this book.

TO LEARN MORE

Cannons, Helen Cox. *Clouds*. North Mankato, MN: Heinemann-Raintree, 2015.

Delano, Marfe Ferguson. *Explore My World: Clouds*. Washington, DC: National Geographic Children's Books, 2015.

McKinney, Cody. *What's the Weather Outside?* North Mankato, MN: Cantata Learning, 2015.

Meister, Cari. *Kit and Mateo Journey Into the Clouds: Learning About Clouds*. North Mankato, MN: Capstone, 2014.